i'm grey.

Sarah eckroth.

this book is for all of those who may feel lost,
and maybe don't want to be found.
it is for those who love and hate.
for those who are strong and tall,
yet quiet at times and can get lost in their own universe.
it is for the people who forgive and forget too easily,
but hold a grudge in the back of their mind.
for those who are not afraid to stand up for themselves,
but at times can forget their worth and have to reteach
themselves to be kind to not only others, but themselves too.
it is for easy going people that can't be pushed around.
the people who everyone goes to for help,
when they might need it most.
for people that are not exactly jocks, nerds, and
everything you see
around in this crazy world full of specific molds
we must all be.
not a total outcast, they see their skin, yet feel invisible.
for those people who do not fit into one category,
this book is for you.

i hope you find peace in being grey too.

i am happy and sad all at once.
i love and i hate.
i am somehow both positive and negative.
i am an introvert and an extrovert.
i am such a cynical person,
yet also positive about the things yet to come.
i am both of everything.
i am both yin and yang.
not defined as black darkness,
or as pure and fresh as white.
i am grey.
and i am okay with that.

-i am grey.

i am the sunshine,
the rain,
and the flowers that grow

-the universe is within you too

i know i shouldn't overthink,
but that's all i've become.
constantly worrying until i feel sick,
about the things that have yet to come.

-my fever soars

as the sink drips,
every drop,
every splash,
mimics my tears.

-*splish, splash*

my pronunciation isn't as defined as i'd like it to be.
no, along with worrying about if my hair is parted
correctly,
if i am staring too much,
if my hands are too sweaty as they shake my hand politely,
i have to worry about having my brain thinking too fast,
mixing up the syllables and phrases constantly.
i am a worrier, and my brain
doesn't help me.
my mind goes much faster than my mouth,
and i wish that people could understand that about me.
i have many stories to tell, speeches to preach,
but i can't ever get them out of my crowded brain,
because i'm afraid of misspeaking.

-a talking mess

i hear voices tell me i'm nothing
i know that isn't right
i know they aren't real
i know they aren't there
but i can't help but believe them

-you can't control me, the voices in my head

baths soothe me.
everyone speaks about how baths are gross,
you must only shower!
you will stay dirty if you go in a bath!

but they comfort me,
laying in a pool of my thoughts and
finally feeling relaxed with myself.
it may not be the cleanest as you say;
but it cleans my dirty conscious

-soap and water

carrying the weight of my worries,
and everyone else's around me
it is who i am.
i apologize for wanting the best result possible.
i'm sorry that the best is
never enough
i am a worrier of my
thoughts,
and desperately trying to be a warrior

-weight

this isn't right.
i deserve more.

-do not settle for less

nobody could love the sad girl

-sad romance

i desperately wanted a forever,
especially with you.
but something didn't feel right.
a little knot,
a little feeling in the depths of my stomach
reminded me of my worth

-i strive for more

everything in my body feels so heavy.
it hurts to move
to breathe
to be

-5:53 pm.

i'm quite odd.
i get tongue tied and feel so self conscious when
i talk to my friends and people i know.
but when it comes to a total stranger, i feel the words pour
out
of my mouth with ease.
a new certain type of hidden comfort comes out.
i love meeting new people,
it's when i feel the most like myself.
a new comfortability in my body emerges,
and i will always ask a stranger how their day is
just because
i can.

-quirky strangers

"you're too young to be sad,"
"oh, you don't know what heartache is!"
"you're so young, you don't even know what love is."
well, you see, i didn't realize that we only were given
emotions on our 35th birthday.
i was too young and naive to understand that all these years,
i've simply had no emotion.
what is love?
what is sadness?
ahh, guess i'll find out when i'm fifty,
because that's apparently the age where you start
developing a mind and feelings.
silly me,
so young,
so naive.

-early ages

i am here, and he is there.

i wonder if we dream of the same things.

-do you dream of us too?

but what can i do?
i need to change the
world.

-be the change

nobody understands.
and for that, i am grateful and also unlucky.
i want to be understood, but i also want to be unique.
i enjoy being different; standing out in the crowd.
i like being noticeable, but i don't like being alone.
i am a crowd, and also by myself,
all wrapped up into one.

-crowded rooms and empty hearts

i'm so tired of trying to sleep every single night,
with no luck.
i see you when i'm awake and feel nothing, but
somehow when i see you in my dreams i wake up
 heart broken.
i don't know if i'd rather feel nothing, or be heartbroken.
but they both mean the same to me.
it isn't fair that you're off living your life, happy as can be,
and i'm the one left not being able to sleep.
you robbed me from happiness,
hell, you've robbed me from my sleep.
i just want to go back to be able to be counting sheep.

-always tired, never sleeping

people always see me as a happy, bubbly person.
and i truly do appreciate that.
but when they say i don't understand sadness,
i wish they knew.
but instead, i keep a smile on my face,
and keep laughing like there's no tomorrow.

-fake smiles and teary eyes

i chew my nails,
i overthink,
i am a picky eater and never let my food touch.
but by far my worst bad habit
is you

-bad habits

i am so obsessed with the fact that there are parts of the world
i've never been to. there are people i've never met,
and cities i've never discovered.
on my worst days, this is what gets me to the next.
because maybe, just maybe, i'll be happier in europe,
my heart will be full in africa, my soul will win in china,
and i will walk with purpose in australia.

-*wanderlust*

i love being unique. i love not fitting in.
i do not cave to society's norms, because i know
i'm not like them. but it is the most comforting
thing that when
i fall asleep at night, there is someone just like me
elsewhere,
with a different body, a different set of eyes
to see the world with, with different experiences,
but the same thoughts,
and same kind heart.

-it makes me know that i am not alone

where do you want to live?
the only answer i can ever give is simply
elsewhere.

-i can't wait to find you there.

it frustrates me knowing there isn't a distinctive word
that means something more than love.
no, i do not love you. it's something more than love.
the way i feel doesn't fit the criteria of love,
because it's much more than that.
i feel the way of a word that doesn't exist,
but means everything.

-you are everything.

i used to be a desert, desolate and bland.
but i've learned to love myself and to let flowers
grow.
i've allowed myself to replant
and seed places in my body where i've been hurt,
and i'm more of a rainforest now.
i understand i am hurt, but i'm done
just feeling sorry about it, letting myself suffer.
it isn't right.
instead, i tend to my hurt places and treat them with care.
and i have to admit, being a garden feels beautiful.
roses come from romantic heartbreak,
sunflowers from loneliness,
morning glories from all the times i felt beside myself,
with nothing to turn to.
i'm my favorite flower, and i will allow more to bloom
if they need to.

-a new wonder of the world

with sadness in her eyes, she conquered the world.

-the biggest hero

my mind and my heart did not match.
my mind always convinced me that the world
is a terrible place, filled with bad people.
always keep your radar up, because everyone
is out to hurt you. however, my heart was the angel.
my heart made me believe there was goodness
in the world, and that everyone has a good quality,
and a soft spot.
what a terrible thing it was to both be the evil and angel
twin, trapped in one body.
maybe that is why i understand people.
there is a bit of good, and a bit of bad in everyone.
/always have your radar up,
because angels and devils can always be found in one soul./

my heart kept me vulnerable but my mind kept me safe.
i was always careful not to get too close to one person,
but to understand them indefinitely.

-heaven and hell

i do not trust others.

when they say they love me, i accept it,

but i think it is a lie.

why does my mind always have to torture me?

i am always caught second guessing, over thinking,

abandoning positive thoughts.

it hurts, thinking everyone is out to get you.

i need to trust others, and to trust myself.

i'm always the person people come to when they are in need.

i automatically know the correct solution to every problem,

and help whomever in need.

and i love being that person.

but why is it that i can help others, but never myself?

i think and i think.

trust is key. and if i do not trust myself,

i cannot become better. i know i am loved.

i am getting better.

i trust myself when i say on my worst days,

tomorrow will be better.

and somehow; it always is.

-self trust

i need to understand desperately that i
can only make myself better.
i am thankful you are here, and you
make the bad days better,
but you are not my medicine.
i must find that on my own, for a heartbeat,
2 eyes, and a smile that could kill
does make me feel better, but isn't my cure.

-human potions are not cures

when the first tremble of my body happened,
i knew an internal earthquake was bound to happen.

-earthquakes from within.

i don't have a specific identity.
i'm not class clown, beauty queen, artistic,
or the quiet girl in the back of the room.
i'm loud, i'm quiet, i'm antsy, i'm sarcastic,
i'm kind,
i'm an everything. i want to be something,
but i don't fit into a category.
i wake up happy, and go to bed sad.
i feel beautiful some days,
others i can't look in the mirror.
what type of award do i get if i'm an everything
and a nothing?

-tell tale of being an everything

it was a good morning.

no, the birds weren't chirping as sun shone

brightly through my window.

no, i didn't dress up and elegantly start my day.

hell, i didn't even have breakfast.

but, when i woke up this morning i laid in bed

in the darkness as the light of day started

to creep through, and felt at total peace.

no matter how hard the day is,

i go to bed at night, hoping that tomorrow mornings

feel like this one.

even though it may feel impossible

sometimes,

sometimes they come.

i am so thankful for the morning.

-crawling out of bed to a new day

i think the worst feeling imaginable
is feeling someone change.
not in a good way of course,
but change to be someone they're not.
someone so obsessed, who loved you so much,
suddenly doesn't answer your calls,
has a new ego.
suddenly you're left there late at night
wondering
if you have changed. you tear yourself down,
and you break.
that is not okay. just because someone else changed,
doesn't mean it's your fault.
that is not your poison to pick.
it is the worst feeling to feel someone slip
away from your fingers,
but don't dumb yourself down
or drive yourself crazy.
they'll turn back to who they were on their own,
not because you spent the nights crying
if you were good enough.

-it isn't your choice to change someone

she was as pure and beautiful of fresh fallen snow,
but in reality that girl was nothing but black ice.

-winter

i write about you,
but my poems are about me.
you are my writing inspiration,
but my sadness composes the poems.
my guilt picks up the pen.
my feelings pour out on paper.
you can say i write about you,
but you're only a piece of my puzzle.

-composing a poem

something you love shouldn't hurt you, they all say.
but in reality, everything hurts you in one way or another.
you fall in love with the sun.
the rays give your body a new meaning of happiness.
you put on your bathing suit and lay in the sun
to get a little darker,
and soak up some sunshine and happiness.
because after all, summer is where you're
supposed to be happiest.
you lay in the sun to get a new fresh glow,
and the next moment you are red.
your body no longer trusts the sun, for it's taken its trust.
you were promised a nice tan!
and now all it is, is a sunburn and pain!
but you forgive the sun, because you can't stay inside
forever.

you miss laying in the sun and the good tan you once
obtained.
so, you forgive and lay back out on your new
beach towel in the grass.
you lay on your back and stare at the clouds, and
notice their beauty.
that one looks like a turtle! that one is a snail!
your eyes meet the gaze of the sun, OW!
you looked too long! the once beautiful rays
burned your eyes,
for your stare was too intense. strike two.

but then again, you forgive the sun.
after the pain of sunburn, of burning your eyes,
you miss the warm glow and go outside once more.
how are you supposed to live without it?
even though it has hurt you numerous times,
you need the sun in order to live.
you have a great tan now, and haven't looked
the sun in the eyes for too long. you've learned
your lesson! only to find, you now have skin cancer.
the rays that require you to live and give you energy
has hurt you once more.

you see, how ironic it is?
something you absolutely love and need in order
to survive, hurts.
whoever says that love shouldn't hurt, is wrong.
love needs to hurt a little bit.
as you head to the beach for a road trip, it starts to rain.
you curse and you're so damn mad because the rain has
spoiled your plans!
how can you possibly have fun when it's raining?
after, a drought hits. the sun kills your beautiful garden
of sunflowers.
too much sun killed your sunflowers, ironic.
your grass is no longer green but turning brown.
the earth is looking dull, and all you want is
to get rid of the sun's rays and bring back the rain.
the rain comes, it always does after a while.
you are so happy to see everything come back to life,
and your grass turn the vibrant green again.
you fall in love with the rain, instead of the sun.

your days inside are so much fun,
watching movies and reorganizing your home,
as you watch your garden spring back to life full bloom!
10 days later it is still raining...
and your gardens overflow, and your town floods.
homes and basements are destroyed.
you wonder how the sun is doing...
because all of the rain swept your beautiful garden away.
the sun comes back, as it always does.
and then the rain.

the sun can burn your sunflowers,
and turn your skin into blisters and rubbish.

the rain can overflow,
and wash away the flowers and homes.

isn't it ironic how we need both rain and sunshine,
but too much of it can be horrible for you?
you fall in love with the sun and the rain,
however, they ultimately hurt you one way or another
in the end.
everything does in one way or another.

to love, is to also feel pain.
love is supposed to be only euphoria,
and have your heart full to its extent.
however, love is lust, happiness,
pains and sorrows all mixed into one feeling.

you love the sun and the rain.
the good and the bad.
because after all, the bad times make
the good times feel even better.
you love and hate love.
ironic, isn't it?

-irony

why is it that when i'm heartbroken, and alone at 3am,
i become a writer? all the pain comes pouring out
onto my white paper with black ink.
i solely become a writer when i'm in pain,
and feeling lost in my own body.
why is it that i can only write when i feel
like the whole world is winning, but not me?
why can i write a little short story when my world
seems to be coming to an end?
they say if a writer falls in love with you, you never die.
but why is the writer allow to die, but not you?
it is my words, and i am forgotten in sadness,
but you always live through love in my heart.
you are my 3am cries,
and my middle of the day panic attacks.
you are my loneliness.
you made me a successful writer.

-pain and misery seeps through my pen

i am constantly surrounded by people who love me,
yet i always feel so alone.
i am in a crowded room of a hundred people,
talking like there isn't a problem in the world, but i feel
like i'm the only one there.
i pass others in the halls, and i am alone.
i am surrounded by all,
yet i stand by myself,
all alone

-alone at last

every day, i look in the mirror and hate what i see.
i am frowning in the mirror,
and nothing ever smiles back at me

-*frowns*

how a writer feels

blank page

goodnight, i am so tired.
but instead of sleeping and putting my mind at rest,
i lie awake.
staring.
thinking.
wondering what i did wrong.
i am always so tired, but i never sleep.
for every moment i'm awake, is already a nightmare.
i do not need to be asleep to have more.

-nightmares during the day

3am is no longer the only tough hour
it's
every
waking
minute

-*morning or night*

i loved the moon, but not even the smallest star loved me.
i loved everything so deeply, with every ounce of me,
but never felt anything in return.
i loved, but was not loved.
everywhere i walked, i fell in love with something new.
i fell in love with the shape of the branches
when you look up at bare trees in winter,
the beautiful vibrant leaves in spring,
and everything in between.
i would walk past an old man on the street,
and fall in love with his kind eyes.
i'd pass a baby in a stroller, and fall in love with
the chubby cheeks.

i woke up every morning for the sole purpose as to be loved.
i dressed nicely to get a compliment from a stranger,
and fall in love with their kind words.
i wore makeup to look beautiful,
so maybe someone might love me.
i exercised until i was exhausted, so i could look
like other girls.
other girls were loved.

all i wanted in life was to be loved.
i didn't think it was too much to ask for.

but for me, love was my five year old fantasy
of asking santa for a unicorn for christmas;
impossible.
you could only dream of it.
it wasn't real, and therefore you couldn't have it.

but one day, i walked down the street,
and noticed something.
there was a different gleam of light on the
tree branches,
and the sun sparkle off the green leaves.
the baby didn't cry, just laughed.
the old man smiled at me with his kind eyes.

and in the end,

i may not have found my soulmate

to live with happily ever after,

but i found the oddest pieces of love,

which made me feel whole.

i look at the moon and the stars differently now.

-love comes in every shape

introvert.

i love being by myself.

all i ever do is get lost in a crowd anyways.

at the end of the day, all you ever have is yourself.

so, get to know yourself,

and spend some time alone.

that's okay. feel the need to be by yourself,

in your own skin.

fall asleep on your own, the bed

is much more freeing and comfortable

all to yourself.

take a mental day, sit home, enjoy your

own souls company.

extrovert.

i hate being by myself.

all i ever do is get lost in my thoughts, anyways.

i would much rather be out in a crowded room,

where people see me.

they give me attention, and we talk as if

there's no tomorrow.

i don't trust myself to sit home alone, doing nothing.

i don't trust that my brain takes over,

and ruins my peaceful night.

i need nights i'll never forget,

and i can't make memories on my own turf.

the greatest times were spent living

dangerously, outside of your comfort zone.

i don't want to fall asleep by myself,

i want someone to hold onto, and

i want someone to hold me back.

i untucked myself from my bed
and laid in solitude
i just sat there and didn't think
i didn't say a word
and for once in my life i felt like it was a brand new day,
and i'm a brand new person.
i shed the skin of last nights tears and felt full and vibrant.
i knew you loved me. but that isn't what this was about.
i loved myself.
it was a good day.

2

i untucked myself from bed.
the sun was shining
the warmth felt nice
but inside i didn't feel a difference
but instead of going back to bed i got up
and continued my day
so i can't complain
i got out of bed today on my own

3

i untucked myself from bed.
then tucked myself right back in
not today.
i'm sorry.

my sleep patterns are nothing but snowflakes,
never the same,
because i am a harsh and cold blizzard

-cold breezes in my soul

neither rain or sunshine,
or the rainbow in between
i'm not badass like a tornado
or as destructive and hated as a hurricane
personally, i relate to the winds
great on a hot summer's day,
dreadful on a cold winter's night.
i'm both bad and good,
and can never stay in one place

-windburnt skin

a bit of romance, a bit of humor.
my life is the greatest tragedy and poem wrapped
up into one.
it is the most blessed scripture,
and consists of blood sweat and tears
some fact, some fiction
my story,
the writers,
is the greatest one of all
but you can never read the full thing you see
for it hasn't been finished yet
there's many more pages to come
i'm not finished with my story just yet
tomorrow will come,
and i'll grab my pen to write down some more

-adding another chapter

my leaves are showing
my mind is growing
spring has sprung
and my days have just begun

-my winter blues are gone

i flood you with seas of love and emotion,
and get nothing but a teardrop in return.
why are you my happiest days,
but consist of rain?

-will a rainbow come?

i overlove.
you may think it's impossible, but it's not.
everything i meet i fall in love with;
it makes life so hard

-too much

sunshine in the middle of the day
you are my shadows

-stop following my every move

impossible to love.

i fall in love so quickly, so hard, so passionate,

and always end up feeling so alone.

it isn't fair having a good heart,

that is always in need of fixing.

make me feel like love isn't impossible

-please

and i know we won't last forever,
and as much as that breaks my heart,
i love wasting my time with you,
before you break my heart.
somehow spending this time with you isn't a waste of all
i know it'll happen, but for now i'll act like it
won't

-stay longer

it's 9:33 am and i am in the school bathroom crying.
i woke up today, and i felt fine.
i heard my alarms, and got out of bed.
i didn't feel like it was going to be the best damn day
of my life,
but i didn't feel like it was going to be the worst either.
just another day on the calendar.
same routine, different day. same schedule.
nothing out of the ordinary.
math class. science. physics. history. sociology.
nothing amazing.

i sit in every class around my friends.

i laugh and joke with them.

they're always so funny.

but by 2nd period, i know something is wrong.

i feel my breathing starting to slow, and my foot
starts to tap incredibly.

everyone looks at me and assumes i am just crazy.

by 3rd period, i sit through class and cannot feel anything.

i am a zombie.

i feel no emotion, i don't laugh at my friends jokes.

4th period, someone asks if i am okay.

for that, i am both grateful and also annoyed.

i am glad someone cares, but also, i don't want
them to ask, because they don't understand no matter what.

i just smile and proceed with my day, and so do they.

5th. i am nothing but a zombie, and i can't pay attention.
i feel one tear fall down my face not because i am learning
about another physics equation, but all i can focus on is
whether
i'll make it through the day or not.
6th. it's another day, spent in the bathroom crying.
7th. people walk in, and i can't let them see me or
know that
i am heartbroken over nothing.
i am in so much pain and crying nonstop for no reason.
8th. i need to pull myself together.
9th. stares in the hallways; at my puffy eyes.
nobody understands that i am walking in the school,
but i am not here. my mind is elsewhere, and i am lost an
want to be found desperately.

-roaming the halls i know by heart

tell me how you feel,

tell me your deepest, darkest secrets.

i don't want to just hear a hello and have small talk.

what was the worst thing that's ever happened to you?

i've got some stories to share too.

-talk to me

just say you're proud of me.

that's all i want to hear.

because everyday i bust my ass trying to be the best i can be,

but never feel it.

i know it's silly to ask, and probably won't change anything.

but i want to hear it still.

i try so damn hard,

that it breaks me down.

anything less than perfect is not okay by me,

because that's what you taught me how to be.

say you're proud of me

-perfectionist

i'm a bit confused.
i was born with the biggest personality,
and i always had a million opinions.
they tell you to always voice how you feel,
but when i do it,
my big mouth gets me in trouble.
but when i say too little, people get mad that i don't care
or i'm too quiet.
do i remain silent, or do i scream how i feel?

-or maybe i should write how i feel

the boredom of seeing the same things
everyday
same people
same everything
i deserve somewhere better

-where to go next

today i learned
my skin will always be here
my skeleton will rise
my muscles will continue to move
and i'll move on,
with or without you.

-*human anatomy*

as gravity pulls to the ground,
it keeps me rooted
love pulls me to you
it is just simple science

-*up in the air*

find me the key
unlock my cage,
set me free,
of all the thoughts traveling through my head

-freebird

i am overjoyed to announce
my future is positive
as i lean away from
your negatives

-electromagnetic field of us